into her eyes

Emma Danaher

Presentation by *BookLeaf Publishing*

Web: www.bookleafpub.com

E-mail: info@bookleafpub.com

ISBN: 9789357619776

First edition 2022

This book of poems is dedicated to my dearest friends Anna Petty, Joshua Lindberg, Nico Greenawalt, Julia Yoon, Mathew Hill, Emilie Ekholm, and Kathryn Morrison, to my favorite high school english teachers Emily Dalton and Shawn Douglas, to my mom, Judy Danaher, to all the dogs I've ever loved, and to myself.

ACKNOWLEDGEMENT

I am eternally grateful and honored to have the people around me. Thank you to my friends for always being there for me and for always supporting me. Thank you to my mom for always having my back and believing in me. Thank you to my teachers who taught me so many things. Thank you to BookLeaf publishing for this wonderful opportunity. Thank you to the world, and everything in it, for being my muse.

PREFACE

I haven't written a poem in 4 years, which was utterly depressing for me. I simply did not have the time nor motivation. So when I saw this 21-day challenge, I jumped at the opportunity. I decided I wanted a fresh perspective and wrote 21 new and original poems in the last 21 days. I was inspired by my friends, by music, by the beauty of the world, and by a few unanswered philosophical questions. This experience was extremely motivating and exciting and I can't wait to share it with all of you!

Thank you very much for reading my poems,
I hope you know that I really appreciate you.

sun or moon

they say that the eyes are the window to the soul.
   as if you can see the passion and
      the fire within another person
        just by making eye contact.
      that fire's alive you know,
    dancing inside you.
breathing and glowing, just as the

you'd think she'd be still, the darkness.
   you admire her from cozy beds
      and look at her with fright.
        alas, she runs and runs and runs.
      she runs up to the heavens,
    past the clouds and the stars
to hug her dearest friend the

these things always tend to happen.
   misfortune and sadness are
      drawn to you.
        just as moths are to light.
      it's raining. and it's still raining;
    it's been raining for days,
and all you want is the

push and pull, yin and yang,
    they can never be apart.
        tides rising over the shore
            and crashing down into the sand
        only to retreat back into the sea
    as the cycle continues;
life and death, ocean and

how would you describe something that's beautiful?
    would you boast of her elegance in a crowded room,
        or would you selfishly whisper your words of praise
            so that she'll never hear you?
        do you bask in her light, ashamed to look upon her?
    full of envy for all the good that she does?
why don't you follow me, as i cherish the light from the

mixed bouquets

let me be your garden.
i'll give you red carnations whilst you feel unloved,
and irises whilst you are doubtful.
i'll grow you hydrangeas for when you're unappreciated,
and chrysanthemums for when you feel sad.
all that i ask is that you remember to water me
in this continuous drought.

upcycled

promise me,
that when all my broken pieces are
scattered all over the floor after i inevitably
fall,
you'll pick up all my pieces,
even the ones that were tossed underneath
the coffee table,
and make me into a mosaic
so that i can be more
beautiful and unique
than i ever have
before.

bittersweet

being content is bittersweet.

it's comfort yet imprisonment.
you've just locked the door and
at the same time you didn't.

it's burying your dreams in pillows
and allowing them to rest.
it's disregarding hope and faith and yearning
to replace with feelings unexpressed.

it's dancing in circles but never getting dizzy
so you don't know when to stop.

you catch yourself yearning for more,
only to remind yourself that wanting is not allowed.

when did you start thinking that way?

break free my dear,
and go fly.

leave behind the bitter
to make room for more sweet.

dreams

forgotten fantasies drift in the void.
will i ever remember them?
do i want to?
i'm ashamed of how many there are.
not ashamed of having them.
ashamed that i can't follow any
without leaving the rest behind.
emptiness mixed with restlessness.
let me do something
let me do something
let me do something;
i want to do everything.
don't make me choose.
i don't want to lose
myself.

am i what i want to be?
am i not me since i haven't done all that i want?

drifting drifting drifting,
seemingly all out of reach.
i choose a direction,

only to regret and turn around once again.
paths start to become overgrown,
each time it's harder to get through.
thorns puncture my arms,
poison ivy claws at my legs.
ducking through branches,
pushing through the brush.

it's getting dark.

i am lost.

no escape

no matter where i go, there is no escape from it.
i try to break free and push my way out but
alas, it is useless and i should just give up.
these invisible barriers are consuming
me in a way i didn't expect them to.
the walls slowly are closing in.
please i don't want to be
crushed by something
i cannot even see.
my time has
come to
a sad
end.

si vis amari ama

please do not ask a flower to water itself.
how can it?

do you wish it despair and sadness,
so that it may cry and keep itself alive?

it's silly to plant a flower
with vile intentions such as those.
don't you want it to grow?

keep in mind that if you want to bask in its beauty,
you'll need to remember to treat it beautifully too.

nightly treasures

as the sun sets and
bids a sweet farewell,
it turns the tree leaves gold.
and so for tonight,
i am rich.

doubtful truth

the sky looked like plastic
and the leaves looked like polyester.
the colors stood out; vibrant and bold.
as if they were painted with
watercolors and acrylics.
i almost couldn't look away
from the harmony and
beauty it created before my eyes.

but the sky looked like plastic
and the leaves looked like polyester.
it seemed simulated and unrealistic,
without flaw or error,
too perfect; too pleasing;
how could anything that beautiful be real,
in a world like this?

and since the sky looked like plastic
and the leaves looked like polyester,
i reached for the sky to see if i could touch it
and when i missed
i reached for one of the leaves
and felt it in my hand.

and it felt like a leaf.

perhaps i am too doubtful.

and all the while
the sky still looks stunning
and the leaves look exquisite
and so i begin to believe
in the beauty of the world once again.

abracadabra

now you see me, now you don't;
i'm a rock in the sea, just trying to stay afloat.
but as that boulder grows and grows,
the easier it sinks, that's how it goes.
and so I am gone, just like magic.

wishful thinking

i wish i was big enough to take all my insecurities
and place them in my palm.
i'll look down at them.
they'll seem insignificant and small.

and i wish i was strong enough
to crush them in my hand
so that they turn to dust,
and are under my command.

then i can blow them all away, right into the wind
to be carried to the shore
where they'll be mixed with the rest of the sand
and be forgotten forevermore.

into her eyes

i stare into her eyes, glowing ruby red.
so hot; so fierce, the danger right ahead.
afraid to breathe, too scared to look away;
captured in eternal fear, i dare not stray
from her gaze. "don't blink"
she seems to say as we fall further into sync
with one another. embers from her fire come
raining from above, burning me til i turn numb.
i begin to shake as i grasp my onyx sword
tighter than i ever have before. aboard
my sinking ship, the water starts to rise.
her roar echoes throughout, drowning out my cries.
smoke clouds my vision as she breathes upon me.
lips begin to quiver as i can hardly see.
she smells of scorching wood and ash;
she sits upon her golden stash.
time is paused, the world we know is gone;
existence remained just for queen and pawn.
hope boils away, escaping out into the air;
and all that's left is shameful, dark despair.
i regrettably accept my sweet demise,
all while staring deep into those dark red dragon eyes.

darkness comes and covers me with a black-stained satin cloak;
i anxiously await the pain from the beast that i invoked.
patience wears thin, when will she attack?
she blinks and i am taken back.
does this mean i won't be mourned for?
is this a victory amongst the war?
do i get to go? do i get to survive?
am i able to come out of this alive?
i see her fire flash around me, igniting all my fear;
her roar is death itself and now it's all i hear.
pitter patter, pitter patter, i feel my own heart racing.
i squeeze my weapon and stand still, embracing
fate itself.

but suddenly her eyes turn green
and i continue onward.

chameleon colors

i turn white when it is snowing
and i turn red when set ablaze.
i turn blue when it is raining
and i turn gold when in her gaze.

blending, blending, blending,
when will this be ending?
conforming is utter agony.
oh, society hear my feeble plea.

let me be purple when you are blue.
i don't want to be like you.
i wish i could be green out there
instead of hiding from your glares.

alas, no one seems to notice and
i end up falling deeper into loathing.
i guess i'll just continue
wearing your suppressing clothing.

a letter to me, a to z

all it takes is one step forward to
begin a new life that's awaiting you.
change is terrifying, i understand but my
dear when you think about it, isn't
everything terrifying? it's time to
fly away from what you know and
grow as an individual. i know from experience that
hating yourself is miserable so
isn't it time to stop?
just take it one step at a time and
know that i'll always be here.
loving anyone takes effort and
maybe you're scared to love.
not because you're heartless
or because you're vile,
perhaps you are just
questioning the concept that's so
ridiculously unfamiliar to you. i
see you in all that you are. i am the only one
that will ever fully
understand you. i'm begging you,
vulnerability is not bad thing,

we have to work together. stop breathing
xenon i have an oxygen mask here for
you please take it and be
zealous in regards to loving yourself.

if you could go anywhere in the
world, where would you go?

if i could go anywhere in the world,
i would go home.

not because my house is where i grew up,
or because i've memorized where
all the good climbing trees are;
but because home to me are my all friends,
new and old, remembered and forgotten.
home to me are the memories i make and relive so often
that make me smile and cry and laugh and hurt.
home is the feeling of peace and a cup of peach tea
as i read a book of poetry while it rains outside.

home is waking up in the morning,
wherever you may be,
and being content with who you have become.

home is loving you for you, and all your scattered pieces
left in the places you loved in and grew in and existed in.
home is knowing that a little bit of you
exists in every step you've taken,

and understanding that
you aren't losing pieces of yourself
but that you're only shedding away the pieces
that do not belong
and finding what makes you whole again.

so when you live,
you are happy,
wherever you are in the universe.

one day I hope to go home too.

yearning

if i had 3 minutes for 3 wishes
i would wish for telescope eyes and eagle wings
so i could fly straight up and see the stars.
and then i'd save my final wish for a cloudy night;
when i'll wish to have dragon lungs
and i'll blow the clouds away,
in order to gaze at the moon

to be an artist

i wish i knew how to draw.

i've always considered myself creative,
but only through words and concepts and ideas.

i could buy the best of paper
and those really fancy pencils,
but it hardly matters.

i can't even draw a line.

oh to be an artist;
how relieving it would be
to know where to draw that line.

the line separating good and evil,
and the line 'tween love and hate.

i wish i knew where to draw the line
between self worth and pride.
to know exactly how much selfishness i need
in order to not hate myself

and to not be full of myself
all at once.

i wish i knew where to draw the line
between my best and being perfect.
to know exactly how much effort i should put in
in order to be proud of myself
and to not be burnt out
all at once.

i wish i knew where to draw the line
between individuality and masking.
to know exactly how much of myself i should be in public
in order to be socially accepted
and to not hide my personality
all at once.

i wish i could draw a perfect line between them,
so that i know where not to cross.
but alas mine are always curvy and oblique,
and i end up jumping back and forth.

and those of you who say go buy a ruler
don't you think i've tried?

i'm sorry to tell you that

rulers don't stop my hands from shaking,
and they don't stop the paper
from getting wet with tears.
rulers don't keep me from ripping the paper
out of anger and frustration,
and they don't keep me motivated to continue.

i'll never be able to draw,
you see.

because i know i'm not an artist.

but maybe one of these days i will be.

i guess we'll have to see.

enticing venom

and when stained glass shatters
into a million pieces
it creates a rainbow on the floor.
but be wary and watch your step,
for too much red can drown the magic.

infinite

i can see the stars from here.

not all of them,
but a few.

the moon shimmers in the darkness,
and reflects in the water beside me.

my ears twitch as frog croaks and
cricket chirps get louder as the night grows longer.

i feel cold.

and small.

probably because i am.

there could be an infinite number of planets,
an infinite number of galaxies,
an infinite number of universes.

it's something we cannot grasp.

we can imagine it,
but forever can't exist in our minds.
we can sit and picture the universe going and going
and going and going and going and going and going and going and

we can trick ourselves into thinking
that we have imagined it.
but the forever in our minds will always end.

humanity cannot comprehend infinity.
and yet we try anyway.

how silly.

we can think about the vastness,
or the emptiness,
or the nothingness.

or we can choose to ignore it.

we can avoid the concept entirely
and focus on the lives we live,
on the only world we truly know.

but in the end,
we are but only a single entity,

drifting along in the darkness.

waiting.

a toast

raise your glasses to her;
the one we hardly speak of.

we embrace her comfort
only when it's convenient
otherwise we scream at her
to disappear and not come back.

she doesn't understand why.

she brings us gifts of
forgotten memories
and peace;
even sacrificing her own privacy
to share her secrets with us.

what else does she bring?
aren't we greedy? aren't we nosy?
we are. and
i'm eager to meet her someday
to find out.

and there are those that try to claim that she is
lonely and it is laughable.

death is not lonely.

she finds us when we are alone
and says that we are not
for she is here to guide us.

but immortality?
immortality seems lonesome. repetitive. exhausting.
what is a beginning without an end?

life gets all the credit.
he's loud and immature and egotistical.
life gives love and hope and good;
yet also hate and doubt and evil.
life is unimaginably difficult and complex;
it's tiresome after a while.

and all the while death is humble;
representing neither good nor evil
but something beyond our comprehension
that she'll teach us later.

and even so we are never grateful.
she takes away the pain when it gets too unbearable.
she gives us a place to rest when we are tired.
she answers questions that life could not.

there's a simplicity to her
that's unfamiliar
yet beautiful
all at once.
a simplicity i wish humanity would notice.

so here's to death herself
and the unknown that follows,
whether it be nothing,
or something,
at least i'm not alone.

if souls exist

if souls exist,
what are they exactly?

well they say the soul is the connection
between the brain and the heart.

so is the soul apart of that,
or is it just the glue?
is it completely independent?
oh god i wish i knew.

and what happens when we die,
our bodies subject to decay,
what happens to our so called souls?
do they disappear or stay?

if souls exist,
where do they come from?
have we created our own souls?
or do our souls create our sense of self?

well they say that our sense of self
is an illusion anyways,
and that the self is just
a sensation of continuity that is
created by the brain.

and if the body and soul are separate,
and our brains are all we are,
what's the soul's real purpose?
do they just float there from afar?

can souls be corrupted?
can a soul be bad?
and can a soul become bad when it once was good?
are our souls our subconscious?
are they the voice within our heads?
and do you think that they would
want to become conscious if they could?

and if souls do exist,
what do they look like as a whole?

why not just look into my eyes;
i hear they're the window to the soul.